IS THIS THE RIGHT COLOR
TO PROVE I DONT HAVE A SHITTY LIFE

JON-MICHAEL FRANK

IT'S SO PEACEFUL OUT HERE
GOOD THING I CAN SABOTAGE
THE AMBIENCE WITH MY
THOUGHTS

AM I MAKING

A DIFFERENCE

PLEASE STOP THROWING
TOMATOES AT ME I'M
TRYING TO TELL YOU I LOVE
YOU

HELP!

I CAN'T GET OUT
OF MYSELF

LIFE IS BULLSHIT

WHEEEE

DRIED THE FLOWERS
SO THEY'LL LOOK UGLY
FOREVER

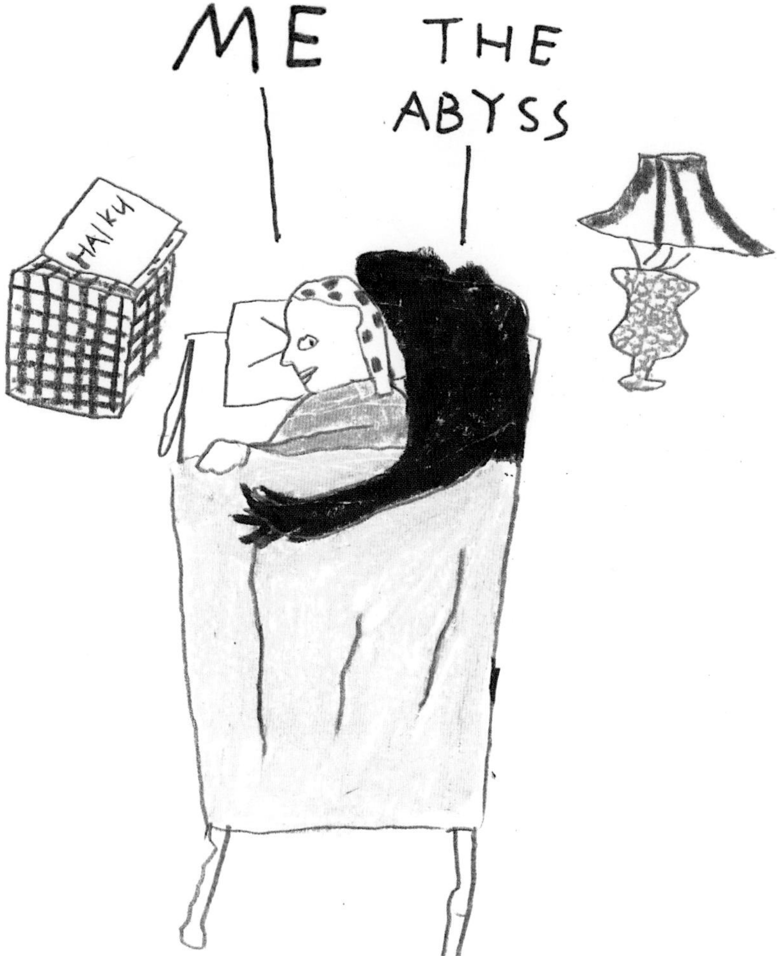
ME
THE ABYSS
HAIKU

I DON'T CARE ABOUT
DEATH
I AM A BUTTERFLY
I KNOW NOTHING

DRINKING CHAMOMILE AND
LAVENDER TEA TO RELAX
NOPE
STILL FUCKED

~~I NEED ANY KIND OF LOVE~~

I NEED AN INTENSELY SPECIFIC LOVE
THAT IF I DON'T OBTAIN WILL
MAKE ME FEEL UNLOVED AND
OVERLOOKED EVEN WHEN I'M NOT

THE TRASH TRUCK CAME
BUT THEY WOULD NOT
TAKE ME

WILL YOU LOVE ME
PROBABLY NOT
BUT It WON'T STOP ME
FROM MISINTERPRETING
OUR RELATIONSHIP

I DIDN'T LIKE ANYTHING
SO IM GOING AWAY

AN ELEGANT LIGHT COMING
IN THROUGH THE WINDOW
I HAVE NO HOUSEPLANTS
SO IT'S UNNECESSARY

I TRULY LOVE YOU
AND ADORE YOU I JUST
DON'T KNOW HOW TO
SHOW IT

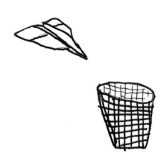

I MUST MAKE SOMETHING
SIGNIFICANT WITH MY LIFE
BUT ALL I KNOW HOW
TO DO IS THIS

DO WHAT YOU
LOVE

I DON'T WANT TO GO
TO WORK I HATE MY
JOB O GOOD A GREEN LIGHT
I WILL BE ABLE TO GET THERE
EARLY AND FINISH SOME OVERDUE
WORK

I HAVE ESCAPED MYSELF
BUT ALAS I MUST GO
BACK IN

MY LIFE IS
WASTED ON
MY LIFE

I THREW A PEBBLE IN THE
POND AND IT MADE A RIPPLE
IN THE WATER
I WISH MY EXISTENCE HAD
AN IMPACT ON THE UNIVERSE

IT DOESN'T MATTER

THE CHERRY BLOSSOMS ARE
NICE THIS YEAR
THE BEST WE CAN HOPE FOR
IS TO DIE BEFORE THE PEOPLE
WE LOVE DIE

I DON'T LIKE THIS
OK I WILL CLICK LIKE

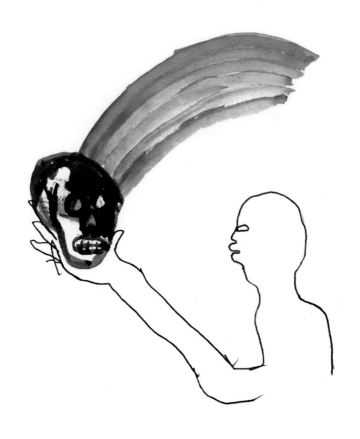

YOU THINK OF SOMETHING
TERRIBLE AND YOU KEEP
THINKING ABOUT IT AND
THEN ONE DAY YOU DIE

I tried to tuRN
the shit INto love
IT DIdNT woRK

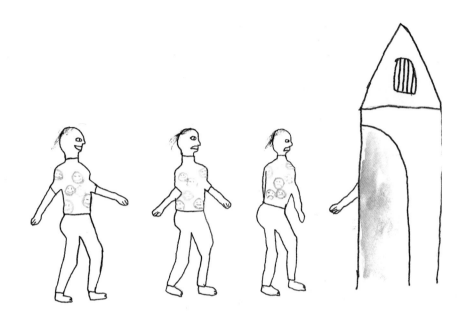

I WANTED TO GO TO THE
STORE FOR MILK BUT I
STARTED THINKING ABOUT MY
LIFE AND I FOUND MYSELF
IN A MENTAL HOSPITAL

$$2 +$$

$$2 =$$

I DON'T KNOW
I'M AFRAID
OF DYING

I WANTED A GLASS OF
WATER BUT THERE IS A
BUG IN IT NOTHING IS
GOING AS PLANNED

I THREW THE BOOMERANG
AND IT DID NOT COME BACK
WILL I EVER LOVE
THE RIGHT THING

IF I LIKE AFFECTION BETTER
THAN COMMERCE THEN WHY DO
I PAY MORE INSTITUTIONS THAN
GIVE LOVE TO PEOPLE IN MY LIFE

THE RIVER IS SO BEAUTIFUL
SNAKING AROUND THE GREENS
OF THE EARTH
WHY AM I MORE EMPATHETIC
TO STRANGERS THAN THE
PEOPLE I LOVE

WILL I EVER LOVE
MYSELF

THIS IS A BEAUTIFUL ROCK
SMOOTH AND VERY PLEASING TO
THE EYE I CAN'T WAIT TO THROW
IT FAR IN THE WATER AND
NEVER THINK ABOUT IT AGAIN

PICKED A MEDICINAL
HERB TO SOFTEN MY
MANIC DEPRESSION IT
DID NOT WORK

WATER LILIES PAINTED
BY SOMEONE WHO DOESN'T
GIVE A SHIT ABOUT WATER
LILIES

I CANNOT FIND A PARKING
SPOT FOR A JOB I DON'T
WANT TO GO TO
TO CONTINUE A LIFE I
WISH WAS MUCH DIFFERENT

THE WATERFALL IS MAJESTIC
AND STUNNING
BUT I HAVE TO PEE AND
I DON'T REALLY CARE THAT MUCH

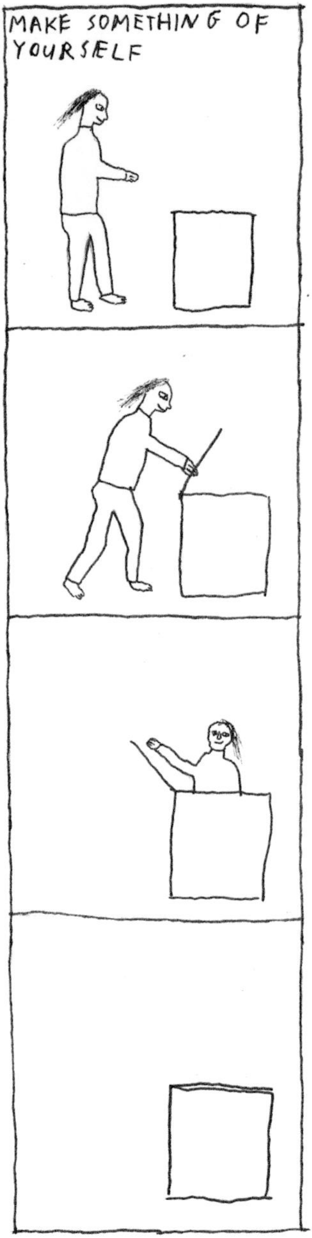
MAKE SOMETHING OF
YOURSELF

SUFFERING

LIVING ALONE WHEN
I THOUGHT I'D BE
MARRIED BY NOW

DOUBT

DOING NOTHING
IMPORTANT

EARTH

KNOWING
NOTHING

PLANETS IN

THE UNIVERSE

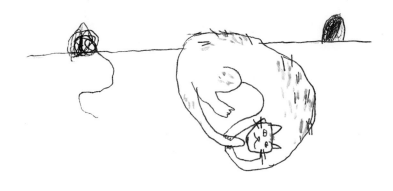

CAT CATCHES OWN TAIL
FOR A MOMENT
BETTER THAN HAVING
TO SPEND YOUR WHOLE
LIFE SEARCHING FOR
VALIDATION AND SIGNIFICANCE

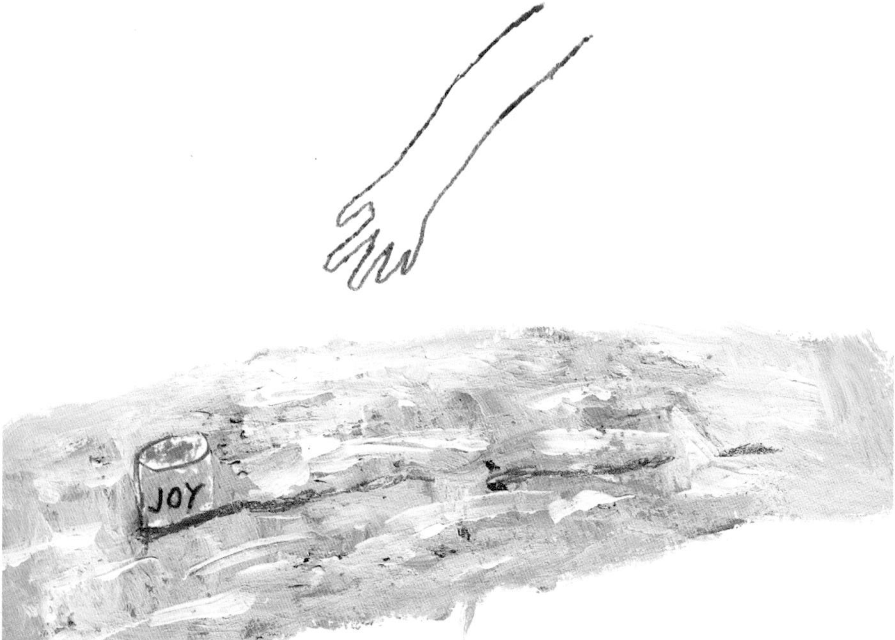
JOY

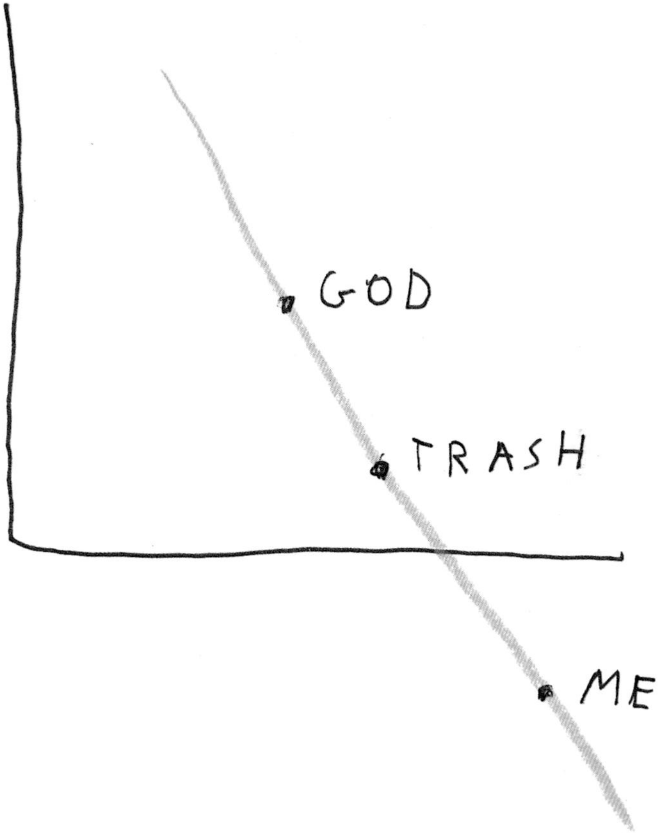
GOD
TRASH
ME

GIVE BACK

I WENT INTO THE
PORTAL LOOKING FOR
TRUE LOVE BUT I DID NOT
COME BACK OUT

CAREFUL
LIFE IS BORING

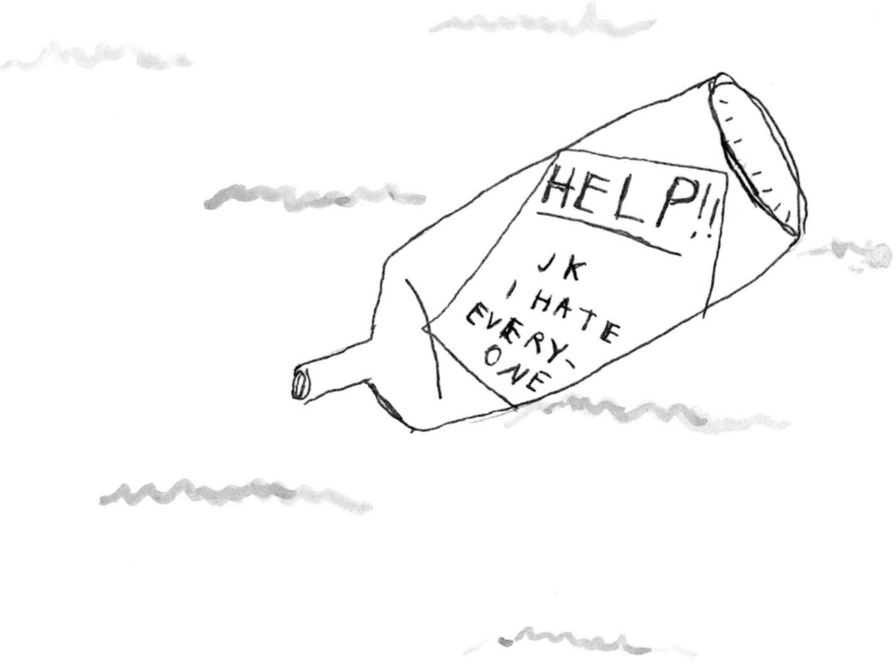
HELP!!
JK
I HATE
EVERY-
ONE

BELIEVE IN

YOURSELF

WHERE ARE WE GOING
NOWHERE IMPORTANT
WILL WE EVER GET THERE
PROBABLY NOT

FUCKED UP PAINTING
MY TOE NAILS GUESS I'LL
NEVER REALLY AMOUNT
TO ANYTHING

AWW
IF ONLY LIFE
WASN`T MEANINGLESS

I CANNOT RELAX

HERE

THE SUN IS RISING
NO THANKS I'M
GOOD

I WILL TRY NEW

THINGS

THE BIRDS ARE COMING NO
THE BIRDS ARE LEAVING
I CAN'T TELL THEY'RE DRAWN VERY
POORLY

THERE MUST BE ONE
THING I KNOW

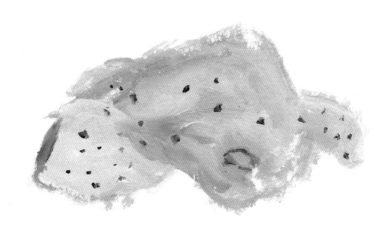

I LOVE BEING AN AMOEBA
I HAVE NO FEELINGS
AND DON'T GIVE A SHIT
ABOUT ANYTHING

WHERE WOULD YOU LIKE
TO GO
TO THE CAVERNS OF HELL
OK

THINKING ABOUT
MEDITATING ALRIGHT I
WILL NEVER DO IT

I LIVE ALONE
I SHOULD NOT HAVE
BOUGHT A SECOND CHAIR

I TURNED THE PLANT AROUND
TO ITS BEST SIDE BUT IT
STILL DOESN'T LOOK ANY BETTER
SAME WITH MY LIFE

I WILL WAIT HERE
UNTIL NOTHING HAPPENS
O IT ALREADY HAS
OK THEN I WILL WAIT
SOME MORE

YOU MISSED THE
BALL BUT KILLED A
BUG NOT BAD

ONE OF THESE DAYS
I WILL DO SOMETHING
SPECIAL AND IMPORTANT
WITH MY LIFE BUT NOT
TODAY NOT TODAY

I FOUND A COCOON
IN THE FOREST
I WISH I WAS SOMEONE
ELSE

I WAS SO CLOSE TO GETTING
MY VERY IMPORTANT DIPLOMA
BUT I DID NOT ANTICIPATE
THIS

PETTING THE DOG TO
NOT THINK ABOUT DEATH
I STILL THINK ABOUT
DEATH

I THOUGHT ID HAVE
MORE LOVE IN MY LIFE
BY NOW

SHOULD I FINALLY UPDATE
MY COMPUTER OR CONTINUE
DETRIMENTALLY LONGING FOR
SOMETHING INTANGIBLE INSTEAD

THE MOSQUITO DIDN'T
WANT MY BLOOD
IT MUST HAVE SENSED
WHAT KIND OF PERSON IT
MADE ME

NOTHING REALLY

MATTERS

I PUT UP A NEW CLOCK IN
THE KITCHEN JUST IN CASE I
FORGET WE ALL DIE WHILE
PREPARING SALAD

THIS DOG CAN BREATHE FIRE
I CAN BARELY WAKE UP
FOR WORK ON TIME AND
I'VE BEEN DOING IT FOR
20 YEARS

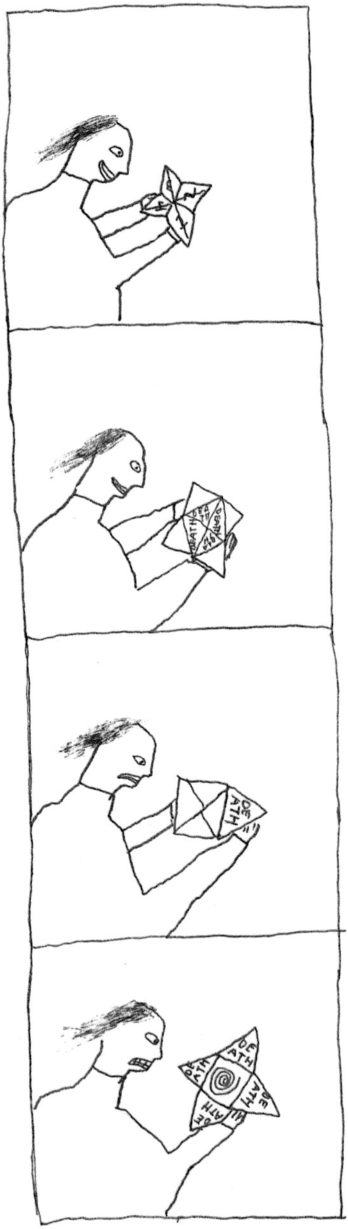
DEATH
DE ATH
DE ATH
DE ATH
DE ATH
DE ATH

WHAT I WANTED
TO BE

WHAT I AM

OUT HERE MY PROBLEMS
DON'T MATTER LOL JK

THE PARACHUTE DID
NOT WORK
O WELL
NEITHER DID LIFE

IM SUPPOSED TO HAVE
A RESUME BUT I'D
RATHER DO THIS

BUCOLIC PATH TO THE
LANDFILL

I WANT A LIFE THAT
MATTERS

I MADE A MISTAKE
I SHOULDN'T HAVE THOUGHT
ABOUT LIFE

I THOUGHT THERE
WOULD BE MORE TO
IT THAN THIS

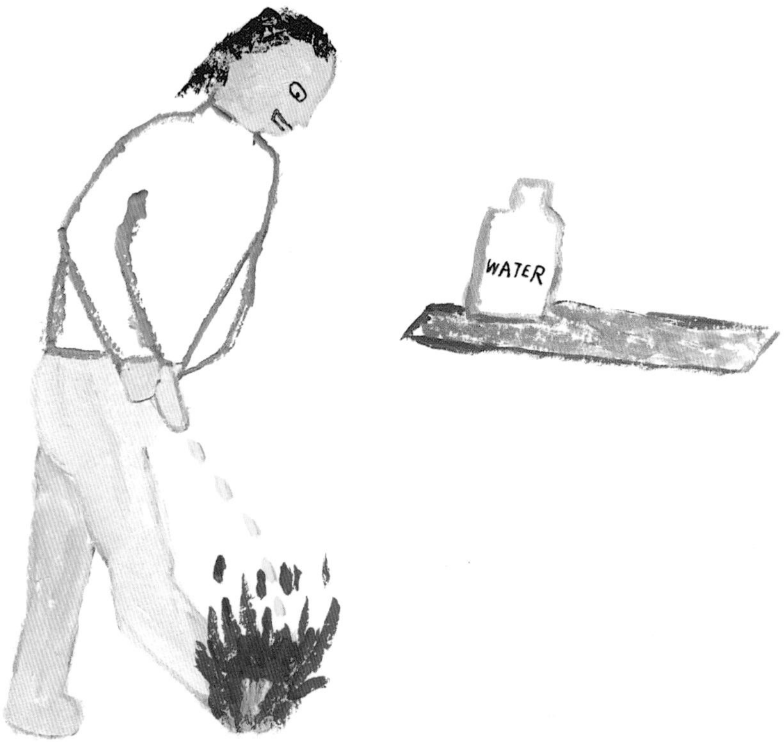
WATER

RELY ON YOURSELF

SADNESS

THE
PLANETS

BIG
BANG

TIMELINE

I TWIRLED THE BUCKET
AROUND AND NOTHING CAME OUT
JUST LIKE MY HEART WHEN
I'M STRUCK WITH A POIGNANT
EMOTION

I WANT TO MAKE
THE MOST OF MY
LIFE

O YES THIS LOOKS
LIKE A GOOD PLACE TO
SPEND THE REST OF
MY LIFE

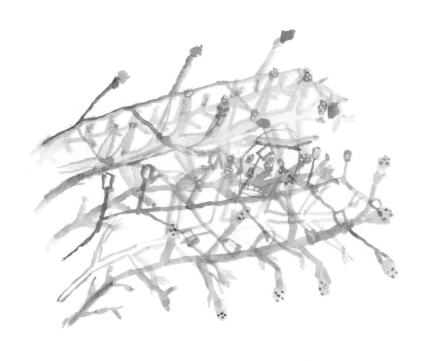

PRETTY FLOWERS BLOCKING
VIEW OF DEATH
PLEASE CUT THEM AWAY

WHAT DAY IS IT

IT DOESNT MATTER
THEYRE ALL THE SAME

NO MORE MAGIC
LIFE IS FINE THE WAY
IT IS

WHY GIVE
LIFE A CHANCE

IS THE JOY WORTH

THE SUFFERING

BEAUTIFUL NATURE BLOCKING
THE VIEW OF VARIOUS
PREDATORS
O MY IGNORANT HEART

SINCE I DON'T GROW
AS A PERSON I LIKE TO
WATCH MY PLANTS GROW
SADLY THEY USUALLY DON'T
MAKE IT THOUGH

I AM LONELY AND

I WANT TO DIE

HOW MANY EARS
DO YOU HAVE?
WHAT?

THE SUBSTANCE OF MY
SANDWICH HAS FALLEN OUT
THE SAME THING THAT HAPPENED
TO MY LIFE AS I GOT OLDER

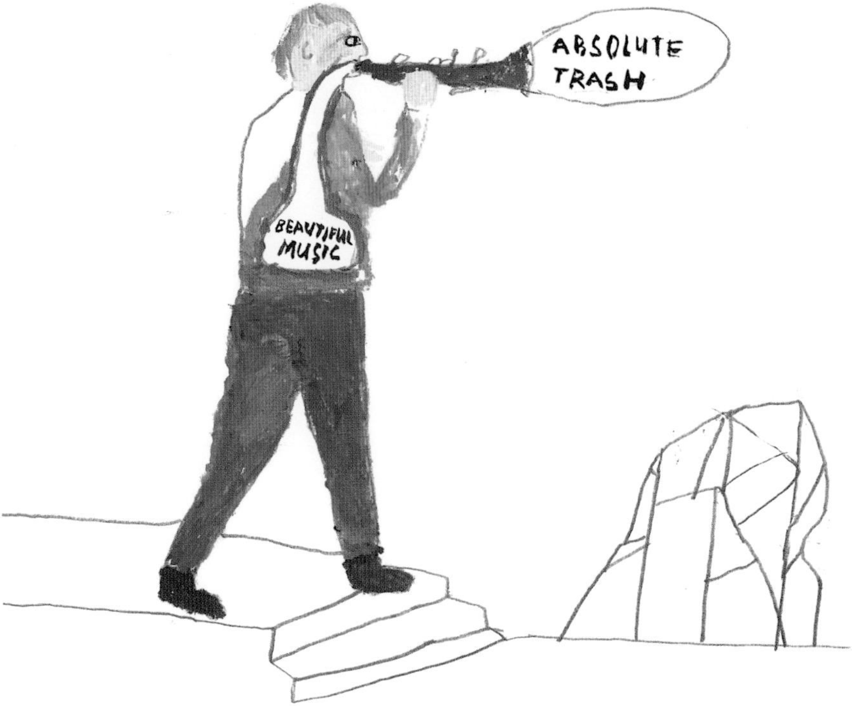
ABSOLUTE TRASH
BEAUTIFUL MUSIC

YOU CANNOT PUT THE
WRONG FOOT IN THE WRONG
SHOE BUT YOU CAN LOVE
THE WRONG THING FOR AS
LONG AS YOU WANT

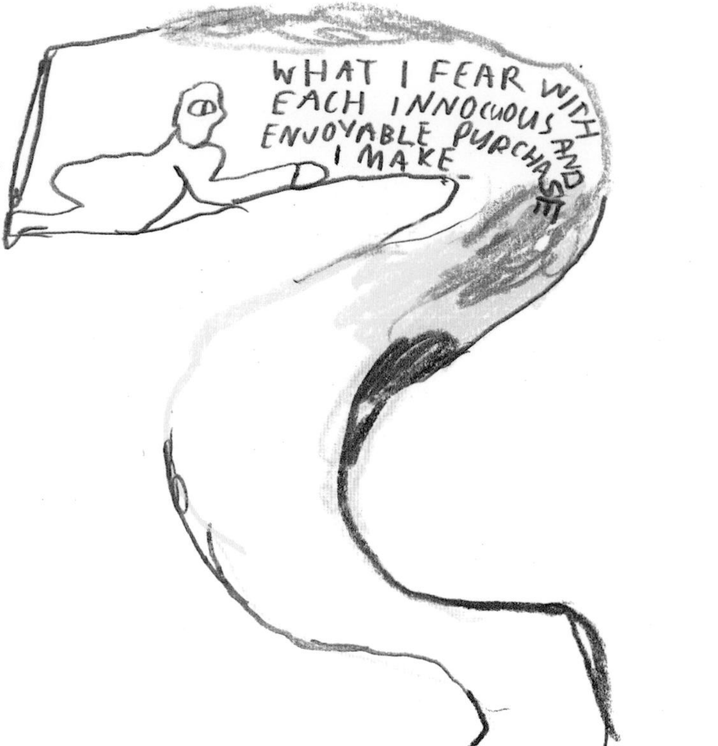
WHAT I FEAR WITH EACH INNOCUOUS AND ENJOYABLE PURCHASE I MAKE
FINANCIAL RUIN

FETCH!
NO THANKS
WHAT'S THE POINT
TO ANYTHING

~~TOILET FLUSHING~~

THE COSMOS

I'M SORRY I'M NOT
A BETTER PERSON THERE'S
NOTHING I CAN DO

WE PUT A SOCK ON
THE CAT'S HEAD AND
HAD TERRIFIC FUN
WHY DO FEELINGS OF
MEANINGLESSNESS
SHAPE OUR DAYS

WHAT AM I
WHY WAS I CREATED
IS THERE A GOD
WILL I FIND TRUE HAPPINESS
WHY DON'T I KNOW ANYTHING

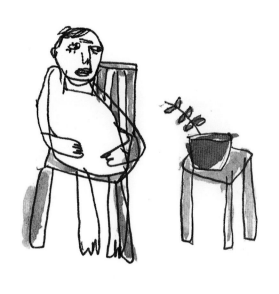

THERE ARE A LOT OF
THINGS TO DO WITH MY
LIFE I CAN'T WAIT TO
DO NONE OF THEM

I AM HOLDING THE
CANDLE
I AM ALSO THE CANDLE
BURNING

EVERYTHING IS
TERRIBLE
BUT I DON'T CARE

WE WORK TOGETHER SHARING
OUR LIVES IN LAUGHTER
CONVERSATION AND COMMUNAL
JOY BUT UNFORTUNATELY
WE ALL DIE ALONE

WHY DON'T BIRDS
LIKE MY BIRD BATH

I GAVE THE PIGEONS
SOMETHING TO EAT BECAUSE
I DID NOT WANT IT
SADLY MY LIFE WAS
MINE TO KEEP THOUGH

I PUT A SEED
IN THE GROUND
BUT NOTHING HAS
GROWN
I GIVE UP

THERES TOO MUCH BEAUTY
IN THE WORLD
IVE HAD ENOUGH OF IT

NOBODY'S ALONE
JK

THIS IS SO MUCH FUN
I HOPE IT NEVER
ENDS

WHO AM I

I DON'T KNOW

WHO CARES

POEM

the best beach house
is never being born
mystical crystals wrapped in toilet paper
if art were life
I'd be shitty at both
seeking a daytime soap feeling
I don't know what to do with
awash in the red curtains
of other people's fantasies
I want my sunburn to be a good memory
sparkling water roaming
in the bristling humidity
at the gully
I throw away my candy wrappers
and dump my spirit into a beautiful weed
you belong to things
as you abandon them

IS THIS THE RIGHT COLOR TO PROVE I DONT HAVE A SHITTY LIFE

Floating World Comics
400 NW Couch St.
Portland, OR 97209
www.floatingworldcomics.com

First paperback edition: November 2019
Printed in China.

ISBN 978-1-942801-73-3